SINCLAIR
COMMIT·THY·WORK·TO·GOD

Ancient Hunting Sinclair
Modern Hunting Sinclair
Ancient Sinclair
Modern Sinclair

CLAN
SINCLAIR

COMPILED BY
Alan McNie

CASCADE PUBLISHING COMPANY
Jedburgh, Scotland

Alan McNie, 1986
© Cascade Publishing Company
Rowandene, Belses, Jedburgh, Scotland

ISBN 0 907614 12 4

Page 1 Explanation:
*The illustrated tartan is Modern Sinclair. The water
colour rendering is of Castles Sinclair & Girnigoe, and in
the foreground is one of the registered plant badges,
Furze.*

Geneological Research:
*Research regrettably cannot be undertaken by the publisher. A
non-profit organisation, The Scots Ancestry Research Society, 3
Albany Street, Edinburgh, undertake research for an agreed fee.*

CLAN
SINCLAIR

Condensed from Clans of the Scottish Highlands,
Thomas Smibert, 1850

The early heads of the house of Saint-Clair were undoubtedly and admittedly Normans; and on settling in the north, they only changed the first part of their name from *Saint* to *Sin* − a curious mutation on the whole, as some wit has remarked. The Saint-Clairs or St Clairs, had been a family of eminence in France even before the Norman conquest of England; and, when they did come to Britain with William the Bastard, they seem to have stood high in the favour of royalty. In the time of Alexander I, or his brother David I, they visited Scotland, and received grants, in the first instance, of the lands of Roslin, near to Edinburgh, and lying within the county of Midlothian. Many traces remain of the possession by them of the Roslin (or Roslyn) property. The castle and chapel, now ruinous, abound in memorials of the house; and the records, also, of the adjoining and ancient Abbey of Newbattle, or Newbottle, mention the name repeatedly. The fifth proprietor of Roslin of the line, styled in rude Norman-French "Guillaume de Seincler", and in common Latin "Willielmus de Sancto Claro", ranked as a baron of importance during the Bruce and Baliol contests, at the close of the thirteenth century. Like too many other Scottish barons, Sir William of Roslin swore fealty to Edward I, and adhered generally to the Baliol cause. His eldest son and heir, Sir Henry Sinclair, followed the paternal footsteps originally, but became in the end a firm friend of Robert the Bruce. A brother of Sir Henry held the bishopric of Dunkeld at the period, and (says Boece) "was a great Fautor of King Robert I, upon account of which, and of his other very noble and heroick dispositions, that king was pleased to call him 'his own Bishop'." The prelate fully deserved the title. On the landing of the English in Fife, AD 1317, Bishop Sinclair threw aside his clerical vestments, armed himself, and, with sixty vassals, marched against the invaders. He met the Earl of Fife retiring before the foe, though at the head of five hundred men. "Who loves Scotland, follow me!" cried Sinclair indignantly; and, with those who did follow, he drove the English back to their ships. Sir Henry "de Sancto Claro" was one of the patriots who signed the letter to the Pope, asserting the independency of Scotland — a letter almost as well deserving of remembrance as the English charter of Runnymede.

Sir William Sinclair of Roslin, son of Sir Henry, formed one of the gallant band of knights selected by Sir James of Douglas to accompany him to Palestine with the heart of the royal Bruce. Sir James, as is well known in song and story, turned aside from his route to join in a crusade against the Moors of Spain, and there perished in battle, fighting valiantly. On the occasion of his death, he had rushed to the rescue of his friend Sir William Sinclair, whom he saw combating desperately, surrounded by Moors, who were "hewing at him" with their scimitars. "Yonder worthy knight will be slain," cried Douglas, "unless he have instant help!" The good Sir James then took from his bosom the silver casket containing the heart of the Bruce, threw it into the press, and exclaimed, "Pass first in fight, as thou wert wont to do, thou noble heart, and Douglas will follow thee or die!" Throwing himself forthwith amidst the enemy, he sank under their swords; and with him fell Sinclair, whom he had sought to save. The casket enclosing the relic of King Robert was recovered by the Scots there present, Douglas having fallen directly above it, as if to guard it even in death. This battle with the Moors occurred AD 1330.

An infant son, also named Sir William Sinclair, succeeded the Scottish warrior who died with Douglas in Spain. This Sir William laid the foundation of the northern and most famous line of the house, by his marriage with one of the daughters and co-heiresses of Malaise, earl of Stratherne, Caithness, and Orkney. That nobleman had himself

Obverse

Great Seal of
Robert the Bruce

Reverse

succeeded to the northern lordships by wedding an heiress (probably) of the Celtic blood. However, the rights to the Orkney and Caithness lordships, it may be remarked, were always confused so long as the Norwegian monarchs held any sway in that quarter of the Scottish dominions. Norway and Scotland frequently supported totally different claimants. The eldest son of the marriage mentioned, Henry Sinclair of Roslin, obtained a recognition of his claim (through his mother) to the earldom of Orkney from Hacon VI of Norway; though such terms of vassalage were imposed by Hacon as showed that a war between Norway and Scotland would have greatly embarrassed the new lord of the Orcades. However, "Henry Seintcler comes Orchadiae et dominus de Roslyne", as we find from "Rhymer's Foedera", had his northern titles admitted also by the Scottish king, Robert III, in 1392; and his son Henry, entitled second Earl of Orkney of the line, acted as chief attendant to Prince James of Scotland, when that royal youth was dispatched by his father, for security, to France. The English seized the whole party (AD 1405), and Sinclair was thrown with the rest into captivity. He seems to have been soon liberated, however, and to have been engaged for several years in negotiations for the release of his young sovereign, James I. Henry, Earl of Orkeny, married a daughter and heiress of Douglas, lord of Nithsdale, by Egidia, daughter of King Robert II. This lady bore to him a son, William, who, about 1417, became the third Earl of Orkney. He was one of the hostages for James I, when allowed to visit Scotland in 1421; and he met that prince at Durham in 1423, on his permanent release from captivity. The Earl of Orkney was Admiral of Scotland in 1436, and, in that capacity, conveyed to France the Princess Margaret, on her marriage with the Dauphin. He founded, in 1446, a collegiate (clerical) establishment at Roslin, for a provost, six prebendaries, and two choristers, and endowed it with suitable revenues. The beautiful chapel which he erected is still sufficiently well preserved to attract universal admiration. The design and workmanship are beautiful − indeed, for a private undertaking, almost wonderful in their beauty. The same William, third Earl of Orkney of his line, held the high office of Lord Chancellor of Scotland in the year 1454. In the following year (August 28, 1455), he received a grant of the earldom of Caithness from the crown, in compensation of other claims,

The Prentice Pillar, Roslin Chapel

Roslin Castle

including, it is said, the lordship of Nithsdale, his mother's heritage. He did not formally resign the Orkney title, nevertheless, until the year 1470, when it was ceded by him to the crown in consideration of various grants of land in the north, and other regal concessions.

The Sinclairs date their proper accession as Earls of Caithness from the year 1455; and indeed they so stand on the books of Parliament at the Union. William, first Earl of Caithness of the Sinclair family, married Lady Margaret Douglas, daughter of Archibald, fourth Earl of Douglas; and, secondly, Marjory, grand-daughter of the Earl of Sutherland. For some doubtful reasons − seemingly because the Douglases stood at variance with the crown about the period, and from the superior influence of the Sutherlands in the north − the son of Lady Margaret Douglas was set aside in the order of titular succession, and in his place, the son of Marjory Sutherland became the second Earl of Caithness. His sire resigned the earldom to him during life, and the king confirmed the cession. The proper apparent heir, William of Newburgh, was well endowed, however, and founded the existing family of the Lords Sinclair; and that Lowland branch of the house, therefore, perpetuates the line of its oldest male representatives. From Sir Oliver, another (and by some styled senior) son of the house, sprang the later Lords of Roslin. William, second Earl of Caithness, fell at the Battle of Flodden in 1513, with his sovereign, and so many others of the Scottish nobility. He had wedded a lady of the house of Keith, who bore to him his heir John, third earl. The confusion resulting from conflicting claims to the Orcadian Isles appears not yet to have fully terminated, since the said John endeavoured to seize Orkney by the strong hand, and was defeated strikingly (AD 1529) by the islanders. He fell in battle on the occasion, with not less than five hundred of his supporters. George, his son, succeeded as fourth earl. He followed a custom very common in those days with men who felt insecure in their possessions and honours. The earldom of Caithness was formally resigned by him into the hands of King James V, who granted a new charter thereof to the consigner's heirs. George, earl of Caithness, had the appointment of justiciary for the whole of the extreme north of Scotland − an almost irresponsible situation in those days. If we may judge, however, from his conduct on the mock trial of the Earl of

Bothwell, for the murder of Henry Darnley, the judicial office would not on the whole be abused in his hands. On giving a verdict acquitting Bothwell, Lord Caithness protested, for himself and others, against being blamed for that decision, seeing that no accuser had appeared to sustain the indictment, and no formal proof had been brought forward of the crime. What indeed could he, and such as he, do else in the case? Queen Mary herself had fallen completely into the hands of Bothwell; and the fact seems to us to constitute the best apology for her acts at this eventful period of her life. Did not Morton, Ruthven, Lindsay and many others of the barons who raised their voices most loudly against the Bothwell marriage, in the sequel put their names to a document advising that very union, and authorise it fully by their signatures? Mary was then only twenty-five years of age. When powerful nobles yielded so slavishly and ignominiously to the influence and menances of Hepburn, can we really wonder much that so young a woman was dunned and stunned into compliance by his audacity? If privy beforehand to the murder of Darnley, indeed, her conduct would be inexcusable. But the probability is, that, if aware of anything planned to his injury, she knew only of apurpose of dethronement. Bad enough it might be to yield even to that proposition; but many, very many circumstances must be taken into account, ere we judge severely of the conduct of Mary of Scotland.

George, fourth Earl of Caithness, died in 1582, and was succeeded by his grandson, another George, fifth peer of the name. From the fourth earl and the son who predeceased him, descended also the Sinclairs of Mey, Murchil, and Greenland, to be more specially noticed afterwards. The contests for superiority betwixt the Sinclair and Sutherland (Gordon) families, in which the Mackays, Gunns, and other northern septs shared largely, had long raged with severity, in spite of intermarriages intended to produce quietude. Probably with such a view the fifth Lord Caithness wedded Lady Jean Gordon, a daughter of the house of Huntly, and, dying in 1643, was succeeded by George, his great-grandson, who married a daughter of the Marquis of Argyle. This union was unproductive of issue, and the Caithness earldom seemed on the point of passing out of the hands of the Sinclairs. George, sixth Earl, actually assigned the title away to Sir John Campbell of Glenorchy, in consideration of certain large sums due

Mary Queen of Scots

by him to that personage. The debts of the earl are said to have amounted to a million of merks, a sum enormous for the age. By this singular disposition (of date 1672), all the titles, possessions, and jurisdictions of George, sixth earl of Caithness, were devised to Sir John Campbell, the latter binding himself to take the name of Sinclair. On the death of the earl in 1676, accordingly, Sir John took up the Caithness title, and even got himself confirmed therein by certain patents and charters. But the heir-male of the Sinclairs, George of Keiss, did not put up quietly with this strange alineation of his family honours. Taking the opportunity, when Sir John Campbell had gone to London (AD 1677) to obtain the royal recognition of his claims, George of Keiss gathered together a strong band of Sinclairs, and forcibly seized on the Caithness lands. His adversary obtained an order for his ejection, but this proved to be a matter of some difficulty, and was not fully accomplished till the summer of 1680, when Campbell in person went north with a numerous military force, obtained from the Scottish Privy Council. He encountered the Sinclairs in a regular battle at Old Marlack, and defeated them. Though he thus secured possession of the estates, however, the right of George Sinclair of Keiss to at least the family title was so clear and undeniable, that the Privy Council found themselves constrained to acknowledge his claims, and he took his place among the peers of Scotland in 1681, as seventh Earl of Caithness. Each party then charged the other with a host of delicts, such as "fire-raising, murder, treason", and the like peccadilloes; but neither of the two underwent a trial, and the matter ended by Campbell being created Earl of Breadalbane, and the Earl of Caithness being reinstated in his proper patrimonial estates of Keiss, Tister, and Northfield, of which the sixth earl, it was decreed, had not had the power to dispossess him. However, George, seventh Lord Caithness, died without issue in 1698, and the pecuniary claims of Breadalbane became again valid in most respects.

By this unlucky business the Caithness earldom received a fatal blow, being shorn permanently of great part of its contingent possessions. The title, nevertheless, found a legitimate owner in John Sinclair of Murchil, descended from a grandson of George, fourth earl. John, eighth Earl of Caithness, took his seat in parliament in 1704, and died in the following year, leaving, by his lady Janet

Taymouth Castle, Breadalbane seat

Carmichael, a son and heir, Alexander, ninth earl. This nobleman left at his decease, in 1785, but one child, Lady Dorothea, married to James, second Earl of Fife. In this instance, the remaining Caithness properties received a fresh scattering. Dorothea, countess of Fife, left no children, and, after a legal contest, Sir John Sinclair of Stevenston (and Murchil or Murkle), a baronet of Nova Scotia (1636), inherited much of the property of the ninth earl, according to the entail. But he did not become Earl of Caithness. The old comitial title reverted once more to a collateral branch, descended from Sir John Sinclair of Greenland, third grandson of the fourth earl, and founder of the Ratter family. It is odd enough that this Sir John had five sons, four of whom held the Ratter estate in succession, and but one of whom left an heir of his body, he also being an only child. The fourth from him in descent, William Sinclair of Ratter, was served nearest heir-male to the ninth, and became himself the tenth Earl of Caithness. His son, John, succeeded as eleventh earl in 1779, and, after serving with distinction in the American War of Independence, died suddenly in London, unmarried, in the year 1789.

Again did the Caithness title seem in peril of extinction. But again was a lawful proprietor of the honour found, in the person of Sinclair of Mey, whose ancestor had struck off from the main line so far back as about 1550, being a son of the fourth earl. The first of the Mey branch, William Sinclair, was chartered in several portions of the Caithness property, and left them to his eldest son, who acquired some note from killing an Edinburgh bailie in a riot of the High School boys, in 1595. He received a remission under the Great Seal for the deed. A second son of Mey, Sir John Sinclair of Dunbeath, acquired considerable wealth as a merchant, and was created a baronet in 1631. That title fell to the line of Mey, it is held, but Dunbeath is still represented specially by a baronet (date of creation 1704). The eighth in descent from the first personage of that line, namely, Sir James Sinclair of Mey, added to the singularity of the successions to this peerage, by being honoured with the title seemingly against his will. Probably he declined taking it up from the inadequacy of his fortune to sustain it in its ancient grandeur; but the freeholders of Caithness, who appear to have been disputing about the county election in 1789, took an objection to his remaining on the roll of voting commoners,

Bothwell Castle

Flodden

on the ground that he was *de jure* a peer of the realm. The Court of Session allowed the complainers to prove that "Sir James Sinclair of Mey had succeeded to the earldom of Caithness". A petition was actually preferred on his side against this decision, and answers followed answers in the case. However, Sir J. Sinclair in time succumbed, and allowed himself to be a lord, the twelth of his line. He was elected one of the representatives of the Scottish peerage in 1807, and also nominated lord-lieutenant of the county of Caithness. By his lady, Jean Campbell, of the house of Barcaldine, his lordship left a considerable family of sons and daughters. He died in the year 1823.

Fate, if the term may be used with propriety, appears not to have been very willing to allow the Norman lords of the St Clair house to occupy permanently the lands of the Gael. But, indeed, the Lowland branch of the house underwent various similar chances; and its honours, in reality, lay dormant for many years. As before mentioned, William of Newburgh, eldest son of the first earl of Caithness by Lady Margaret Douglas, was somewhat strangely superseded in the paternal succession in the north by the son of a Sutherland marriage. William of Newburgh, however, unquestionably the true heir of the St Clairs, did not receive the ancient Roslin lands, though certainly endowed with considerable possessions in the Lothians, and filling an eminent place in society. His sister-german had the honour even of an alliance with the blood-royal, wedding the Duke of Albany, second son of King James II. His heir, Henry, again, was created Lord Sinclair by James IV in 1489, and following that monarch to the field, fell with him at Flodden. By Margaret Hepburn, of the powerful house of Bothwell, he had William, second Lord Sinclair, who is shown by charters to have held lands in the shires of Aberdeen and Fife, and to have wedded into the family of Marischal. His son Henry was predeceased by James, master of Sinclair; but the latter left a family, three sons of which became barons of Sinclair in succession. The line seems here to have been threatened with a fatal pause; and still more imminent grew the danger, when John, heir of the last of these sons, and seventh baron of the house, died, leaving an only daughter, Catharine. However, this lady wedded John Sinclair of Hermandston, a near male descendant of the family, and their son Henry became the eighth lord.

But the eldest son of Henry was attainted in 1715, and, as he left no issue, the second son became clearly entitled to the peerage. He never advanced his claims, probably from the same motives which actuated Sinclair of Mey in the Caithness case. At his death in 1762, the descendants of Matthew, fourth son of Sinclair of Hermandston, had a right to the baronial honours. They still remained unassumed, nevertheless, up to the date of 1782, when the House of Lords, being appealed to, adjudged the title to Charles, great grandson of Matthew Sinclair. Reckoning all the parties who might have borne the dignity, Charles has usually been considered the thirteenth Baron Sinclair. He served in the army, and sat in the House of Lords as one of the representatives of the Scottish peerage.

In regard to the main lines of the Sinclairs, we have here followed the most reasonable account, viewing the Lowland families of the name as founded by two brothers, William (ancestor of the Lords Sinclair) and Oliver, progenitor of the lairds of Roslin. Some genealogists hold the latter branch to have been the oldest; but Nisbet distinctly relates, that he had seen a remarkable family contract, of date 1481, in which Sir Oliver Sinclair of Roslin dispones all claims over certain Lowland estates to "his *elder brother* William" (of Newburgh), and further binds himself, that "should there happen any plea betwixt the said William and his *younger brother,* for the earldom of Caithness, he (Sir Oliver) shall stand evenly and neuter between them, as he *should* do betwixt his brothers." This deed goes far to establish the fact of the singular division of property among the Sinclairs, already mentioned, whereby the younger got the honours of an earldom, and the others lands merely − perhaps the best and richest, but not possessing the same titular rights and honours. Notwithstanding this piece of evidence, the candid Nisbet observes, which of all these families is the oldest he cannot well say.

Castles Sinclair & Girnigoe

Some Associated Names

Associated names have a hazy history. Sometimes they had more than one origin; also clouding the precise location of a particular surname might be that name's proscription or of course a migrant population. Even the spelling of surnames was subject to great variations, shifting from usually Latin or Gaelic and heeding rarely to consistent spelling. In early records there can be several spellings of the same name. Undoubtedly contributing to this inconsistency is the handwriting in official records, which was often open to more than one spelling interpretation. There is no official registered list of sept names but the names listed have clan association.

CAIRD   Caird is the Anglicised form of 'Clann na ceairde', the Gaelic name for Sinclair in Argyllshire. In 1275, Gilfolan Kerd was arrested in Bristol for piracy. In 1382, Adam Kerde of Fyvie (7m SE of Turriff) was excommunicated. John Kerde was commissioner of Irvine in 1430 and in 1446 William Kerde was a witness in Prestwick. Duncane McIncaird recorded in Glenurcht in 1611 (Glenurquhart — 7m W of Drumnadrochit, Inverness-shire). Robert Kerd made 4 horseshoes for David II in 1343. In 1632 David Kaierd died at Carmyllie. (6m NW of Arbroath.)

CLYNE   From the parish and lands of Clyne in Sutherland and site of a battle between the Sutherlands and Sinclairs. The Clynes were dependants of the Sinclairs who defended them against the cruelty of the Sutherlands of Berriedale. In 1375 William de Clyn held the lands of Cathboll in Tarbat (8m NE of Tain). The bishop of Orkney's secretary in 1390 was named Malcolm de Clyne. William Clyne of Clyne witnessed two seisins of the earldom of Sutherland in 1456 and 1462. His line ended in daughters, one of whom married a Sutherland. In 1662 Alexander Clyne is recorded in Greenland, Caithness.

GALLIE, GALLY   From the Gaelic 'gallaich' which is the Sutherland name for the people of Caithness as being strangers or foreigners. Also thought to be a sept of the clan Gunn who were expelled from Caithness in 1589 and settled in Tain taking the collective name as a surname. The name Gallie is also found inAyrshire where it also means stranger. In 1426 Patrick Gallies had a tenament in Irvine. John Galie and his wife were accused of being witches in 1662 in Bute.

GROAT   The family of Groat were grated a charter of land in Duncansbay, Caithness (1m S John o' Groats) in 1496 by William de St. Clair, Earl of Caithness. Also a common name in Fife, especially in Dysart (2m NE Kirkcaldy) where Christinn Grott and Walter Grote are recorded in 1545 and Henricus Grot in 1571. A clergyman in Wick in 1530 was named Hugo Grot. William Grot was the heir of Malcolm Grot of Tankerness in 1632 (6m ESE of Kirkwall).

LINKLATER   A decidedly Orkney surname, from placename Linklet in Orkney. Lady Isobel co-heiress of Orkney and Caithness married Sir William Sinclair of Roslin; their son became Jarl of Orkney in 1379. In 1424 Criste AElingeklaet was named as a gentleman by the Commons of Orkney. Helen Linklet recorded in Under Failze, Fetlar in 1613 (33m NE Lerwick). Thomas Linkletter in 1634 in Laxford (NW Sutherland). John Linckletter of Housbie (8m SW Lerwick) had William for his heir in 1649. In 1678 Andrew Linklate was a delegate for North Sandwick (5m N Stromness). Peter Linkletter was a quarter master on the 'Bounty' and stood by Captain Bligh in the mutiny.

MASON   From the occupation of mason. A prominent family of this name lived in Orkney in the 16th century. In 1180 Roger Amentarius de Forfar was probably the chief builder of Forfar royal palace. In 1271, Richard the Mason was burgess of Aberdeen. Nicholas Masoun of Stirling in 1360 probably did the sculpture work of the tomb of Robert II. William Maceoun of Berwick received monies from the Exchequer in 1327. The Masons were a notable family in 16th century Orkney.

Bonnie Prince Charlie

Sinclair Country
DETAIL MAP OVERLEAF

The map used below and overleaf is intended basically as a pictorial reference. It is accurate enough, however, to be correlated with a current map. The clan boundaries are only marginally correct. No precise boundaries were kept in early times and territories were fluctuating frequently.

SINCLAIR
CLAN MAP

1 **Ackergill Tower** Ancient Sinclair tower remains in modern home

2 **Berriedale Castle** Only scanty remains of Sinclair castle

3 **Brawl Castle** Ancient ruins with Sinclair association

4 **Dunbeath Castle** Sinclair stronghold perched high above fishing village

5 **Helmsdale Castle** 11th Earl of Sutherland poisoned by Isabel Sinclair

6 **Keiss Castle** George Keiss resisted financial control by Campbells

7 **Mey, Castle of** Sinclair home became Queen Elizabeth, the Queen Mother's

8 **Old Wick Castle** 14th cent. ruin with Sinclair association

9 **Orkneys** (southern tip only shown). Early Sinclair succession

10 **Sinclair & Girnigoe, Castles of** Ancient adjacent ruins

11 **Thurso Castle** Birthplace of agriculturist & statistician, John Sinclair

12 **Wick** Earls of Sinclair are buried in Sinclair Aisle of Parish Church

Pentland Firth
Swina
Lones
Stroma
Pentland Skerries
Dunnet Head
or Dunnet Head
 Windy Knap
Duncansby Head
Dungsbay
Freswick Bay
Keiss
Sinclairs Bay
Castle Sinclair
Wick
Wick Bay
Staxigo
Papigo
Oldwick Castle
Hempriggs
Sarclet
Ulster
Mirligo
Clyth
Clyth Ness
Fors Castle
Seal or Scalk Cave
Lathron Wheel R.
Knockennon Castle
Dunbeath Castle
Borg
Langwell
Berrydale Castle
Ausdale
Ord of Carth
Garth
Cutgoar
Lothmore
Glyn Iush
Dunrobin
Golspie
Tynes R.
Tarbat Ness
Tarbat Castle
M Tarrel
Cathow C
Sandwick
Cowtinade
Cromarty
Nairne

Sinclairs supported Bruce

Bannockburn

Sinclair *by MacIan*

Name of Individual or Head of Family.	Occupation.	Place of Residence.	Age of Head.	No. of Children.		Meal supplied per lbs.	Other Supplies.	Remarks.	By subscribing in this Column, the Parties receiving the Supply agree to work or pay therefor.
				Above 12.	Under 12.				
James Gunn	Do & Fisher	Burrigh	44		6	42		+ Wife in Destitution	Do 4
Arch. Sutherland	Do & Cooper	Ashley	53	2	2	28		+ Do Do / Idle during the winter	Do 5
James Gunn	Mill & Farm	Croft	41	1	4	28		+ Wife Destitute	Do 6
Hugh Mackay	Croft & Fisher	Roadside	38		8	42		+ Do Do	Do 7
Hector Sutherland	Do Do	Forn	40		6	42		+ Do very Do	Do 8
John Nicoll	Do Do	Rhimigin	52	3	3	42		+ Do " Do	Do 9
Widow Jo. Sutherland	Croft	Burrigh	60			14		Do	Do 10
Henry Gunn	Do	Mill & Farm	40			14		Do	Do 11
Will. Sinclair	Do & Fisher	Do	34		2	28		Do	Do 12
Alex. Mackay	Croft	Lochend	76			28		+ Wife Do	Do 13
Wm Cormack	Do	Mill & Farm	72			28		+ Do Do	Do 14
Peter Sutherland	Do	Rumster	65	2	2	28		+ Do Do	Do 15
Cath. Nicoll	Subtenant	Croft	28		3	21		Husband South for work family Destitute	Do 16
Sinclair Sutherland	Croft	Mill & Farm	60	2	2	28		+ Wife Destitute	Do 17
Christian Nicoll	Do	Do	53			14		Do	Do 18
Robert Macdonald	Do	Rumster	34		4	28		+ Wife Do	Do 19
Alex. Mackenzie	Do	Do	53	3		28		+ Do Do	Do 20
Jas. Munro	Do	Bincheilt	40		4	28		+ Do Do	Do 21

1847 Register of Destitute from Ulbster.

Berriedale Castle

Dunkeld Cathedral

Some Clan Notables

Sinclair, Patrick (1736-1820) Patrick Sinclair was born at Lybster, Caithness. He went to Canada with the army and the Great Lakes fascinated him. In 1775 he was appointed lieutenant governor and superintendant of Michilimackinac in Quebec. He organised expeditions against the Spanish in St. Louis and spent all his official funds in keeping the Indians loyal to Britain. The military refused to pay his drafts and Sinclair died impoverished at Lyster.

Sinclair, Sir John *(1754-1835)* Born at Thurso Castle, this eminent Sinclair made a dual contribution to posterity: stimulating writing on a wide range of innovative agricultural themes such as experimental farms gained him a European reputation; compiling the Statistical Account of Scotland *(1791-1799)* was a gigantic task. The latter, although of Scottish content, was recognized as a monumental achievement overseas, serving as a model for other nations. This remarkable man also found time to serve for a long period as a member of parliament.

Sinclair, Andrew (1796-1861) Born in Paisley, Andrew Sinclair trained as a surgeon and was appointed assistant-surgeon in the Royal Navy. He became interested in botanical work and sold and gave many important specimens to the British Museum. In 1844 he became Colonial Secretary and was a shrewd advisor and businessman. He died on an exploration of the Southern Alps in 1861.

Sinclair, Catherine *(1800-1864)* Born in Edinburgh, this talented and prolific authoress, with a social conscience, became internationally popular. *Beatrice* sold over 100,000 copies in England and America. Her works always conveyed a strong moral tone. Within Edinburgh she was a community activist, who launched many projects to assist the underprivileged.

Sinclair, James (1817-97) James Sinclair was born in Lybster, Caithness and emigrated to New Zealand. In 1852 he built the first wooden house at Wairall and became friendly with and did business with the natives. He acted as merchant and banker for runholders. He was regarded as the founder of Blenheim and responsible for fixing the capital there. He was a member of Councils from 1860-74 and largely responsible for the separation of Marlborough from Nelson.

Sinclair, Alexander (1840-1924) A clergyman and Gaelic scholar, Alexander Sinclair was recognized in Canada as an authority on Gaelic language and literature. He was ordained a minister of the Presbyterian church in 1866. He published many books on the Gaelic language and Gaelic poetry. In 1907 he was appointed lecturer on his subject at Dalhousie University, Halifax.

Sinclair, Upton (1878-1968) Upton Sinclair was an American novelist and political writer. His novel 'Jungle' exposed unsanitary conditions in the packing houses of Chicago and caused public outcry. Sinclair was invited to discuss conditions with Roosevelt and an investigation led to the Pure Food & Drug Law being passed. Sinclair became a member of the Socialist party in 1902 and in 1933 he stood for governor of California unsuccessfully. 'World's End' an eleven volume series was designed to give an inside view of American Government between 1913-49. His novel Dragon's Teeth, about the rise of Nazism, published in 1942 won the Pulitzer prize. By his death, Sinclair had produced 90 books earning 1 million dollars, of which the majority was donated to socialist and reform causes.

ACKNOWLEDGEMENT
We are indebted to staff members of the Scottish Room, Edinburgh City Libraries for their generous assistance.

Research work done by Barbara Blackburn has proved valuable and thorough.